LIFE

IN THE

SLOW LANE

Backroad Tours of Northwest Ohio for Sunday Drivers, Bicyclists, and Other Explorers.

Covered bridges, pioneer cemeteries, Indian memorials, nature preserves, old churches, water mills, and much, much more!

by
JEFF AND NADEAN DISABATO TRAYLOR

Life In The Slow Lane is a registered trade name of
Jeffrey and Nadean DiSabato Traylor.

Published and distributed by:

Backroad Chronicles
P.O. Box 292066
Columbus, Ohio 43229

Also available from Backroad Chronicles:
Life In The Slow Lane: Backroad Tours of Central Ohio
Life In The Slow Lane: Backroad Tours of Southwest Ohio

Printed in Columbus, Ohio, U.S.A.

ISBN 0-941467-02-3

To the Strawberry Gang
of Troy Mills Farm

Introduction

This tourbook was written for modern day adventurers who wish to travel the backroads to Northwest Ohio's past and discover a world that lies beyond the freeways and city lights. Whether you are a Sunday driver, bicyclist, history buff, or simply like to roam, you will find many hours of enjoyable and informative touring on these country roads. Ohio's past becomes present as you discover covered bridges, Indian memorials, pioneer cemeteries, water mills, old churches, and other historical points of interest. Our natural heritage likewise is awaiting your exploration in the prairies, woodlands, islands and lakes of Northwest Ohio. To further complement your ramblings, many of the loops also include swimming beaches, campgrounds, picnic areas, and walking trails.

A simple-to-use trip planning guide provides information to help you select your tour, and an Ohio outline map gives you the loop's location at a glance. A historical narrative accompanies each loop description, and information about the various points of interest is provided. County road maps have been used as base maps for these self-guided tours, and each map is clearly marked and annotated. Routes have been selected that offer the best combination of scenery, surface, and low traffic, while connecting the points of interest. Of course, road and traffic conditions are subject to change. Because bicyclists and motorists must share the roads, we urge cyclists and drivers alike to observe safe riding/driving practices, and for cyclists to know their skills and physical limits before embarking on their bicycles. The authors assume no responsibility for the safety of persons using these routes.

Food and drink are frequently, but not always, available along the routes, therefore we find it good practice to carry water and sandwiches — especially when we find a scenic picnic spot! And one final word about country roads — they sometimes have several names, but the road number is usually reliable. When in doubt, counting crossroads and using the map scale are useful tools for the backroad explorer. But if all else fails and you stray from the route, keep your eyes open. There's no telling what you may discover!

HAPPY TRAILS!

About the Authors

Ohio natives Jeff and Nadean DiSabato Traylor are devoted explorers of out-of-the-way places. After completing a 1,600 mile bicycle trip through Ohio, Michigan, and Ontario, they found, like Dorothy, "there's no place like home". Their explorations into the Ohio countryside in search of Ohio's pioneer history and natural heritage have culminated in this unique *Life In The Slow Lane* series. In addition to being chroniclers of country roads, the Traylors established a successful retail business in Columbus' historic North Market, and have been professionally engaged in the fields of mental health and retardation.

Acknowledgments

The authors wish to thank the following agencies for providing information that helped make this book possible:

The Ohio Historical Society

The Ohio Department of Natural Resources

The Ohio Department of Transportation

and numerous libraries, museums, and historical societies throughout northwest Ohio. We are also indebted to many individuals who have contributed to this project in a variety of ways, including Barb Padgett, Vern Pack, Paul and Rita Bishop, John and Ellen Schwab, Joe and Pat Toronto, Dick Helwig at The Center for Ghost Town Research in Ohio, Dr. Sal Lowry, Jane Willman, Tom and Norma Traylor, Marcus Orr at Country Living Magazine, and the many people we have met along the road who welcomed us and shared their knowledge. Thank you one and all.

Abbreviation Key

The following road number prefixes are used in the book: T or TR = Township Road; C, CR, or no prefix = County Road; SR or Ohio Outline = State Route. Extra caution is advised in those few instances where it is necessary to cross or travel a short distance along a state route.

Trip Planning Guide

# Name	Length miles [short loop]		Historical site	Nature preserve	Museum	Covered bridge	Pioneer cemetery	Picnic area	Camping (state/county park)	Swimming	Walking trails
1. Magnificent Metal	29		X			X	X	X	X		X
* 2. Down By The Old Mill Stream	45	(30)	X		X		X	X	X		X
* 3. The Andrews Raiders Ride	25		X				X	X	X	X	X
4. The Crane Creek Ride	39		X	X			X	X		X	X
5. The Tarhe Trek	48		X	X	X	X	X	X			X
6. The Black Swamp Ride	48		X	X			X	X	X		X
* 7. The Great Northwest Ride	47	(31)	X				X	X	X	X	X
* 8. The Winameg Wander	42		X				X	X	X	X	X
9. Island of Stone	14		X	X	X		X		X	X	
10. The Road to Recovery	45		X		X			X			
11. A Savanna Sojourn	34		X	X		X	X				
* 12. Top of the Canal	21		X		X			X	X	X	
* 13. The Fort Amanda Ride	42		X				X	X	X	X	X
14. Red Barn Country	31		X		X		X	X			X

* Camp-Over Option: Two loops leave from same state park where camping is available.

Tour Loop Locations

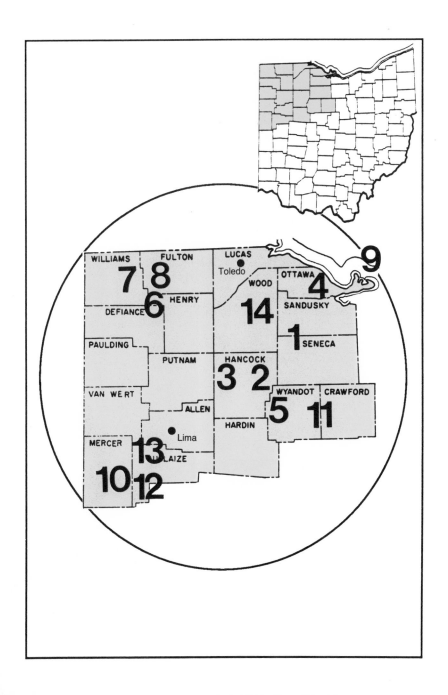

LOOP #1

Length: 29 miles

Terrain: Flat to gently rolling

County: Sandusky/Seneca

Magnificent Metal

This 29 mile ride through the flat to gently rolling countryside of Sandusky and Seneca Counties begins along the banks of the scenic Sandusky River, winds past historic sites from the War of 1812, passes beautiful country churches, and takes the traveler across river and stream on a variety of bridges, including covered and iron spans. The route then departs from the river to cross open countryside on the way to "the world's largest natural sulphur springs".

There is a certain charm, an allure, to the majestic bridges of days gone by. The importance of a bridge to a young community striving for growth is displayed in the scale and pride with which the early bridge builders plied their craft. Far from making a bridge virtually indistinguishable from the roadway, yesteryear's engineers and ironworkers made monuments to their skills, creating structures that towered above their surroundings. With their beams arching high overhead in a constellation of iron, the river rushing beneath in full view, it is an event to cross these wonderful old spans.

The importance of these bridges, whether they be of iron or timber, is reflected not only in their size and scale, but in the struggles that underlie many of them. One bridge on this loop, the Abbott Bridge, is on a site steeped in controversy and tragedy. In 1870, the first bridge built on this site, the Watson Bridge, was erected over the objections of the people of Fort Seneca, who wanted a bridge over the Sandusky River located closer to them. Watson, being a county commissioner, got his way, but an early account reveals that "the bridge was more an experiment than a good job. The timbers were left exposed, and the bridge was not anchored well. When the great hurricane swept over the northern part of Seneca County in June, 1875, blew down the M.E. Church in Fort Seneca, throwing it flat on the ground, it also blew the Watson Bridge into the river in a body, leaving the abutments only".

After the "hurricane", the haggling began again, and while the bickering continued, two men drowned trying to cross the river to vote in a township election. It was then decided to build the new bridge at Fort Seneca. A few years later, a Mr. Flummerfelt persuaded the commissioners to put up some money, along with his, and the Flummerfelt Covered Bridge was erected on the site of the Old Watson Bridge, followed in 1897 by the metal bridge that stands yet today.

Although the metal bridges of the late nineteenth century are now vanishing, the traveler on this loop will pass an even earlier bridge over the East Branch of Wolf Creek. Built in 1851, the Mull Covered Bridge has earned a place on the National Register of Historic Places. By-passed and preserved, the bridge is one of the backroad treasures of Sandusky County.

POINTS OF INTEREST:

1. *Wolf Creek Park*
   The ride begins at Sandusky County's Wolf Creek Park, nestled along the west bank of the scenic Sandusky River on the east side of SR 53. Picnic tables, restroom facilities, grills, drinking water, and nature trails are available, and a camping area is located about one mile south of the park.

2. *Caution: Route Note*
   Be extra cautious as you travel busy SR 53. A narrow berm is available for cyclists.

3. *Hill Cemetery*
   Located on the northeast corner of SR 53 and TR 9 is an early cemetery where the grave markers of John Delong and Jacob King, veterans of the War of 1812, can be found.

4. *Mull Covered Bridge*
   Spanning the East Branch of Wolf Creek on TR 9 is the by-passed Mull Covered Bridge. Built in 1851, this Howe Truss bridge is on the National Register of Historic Places. Photographers may want to take advantage of the view from the replacement parallel bridge.

5. *1875 M.E. Church*
   When "the great hurricane of 1875" destroyed the M.E. Church, "throwing it flat on the ground", this beautiful church was built in its place. The church has not been used since 1975, and now is private property. It is clearly visible from the road as you pass by.

6. *Fort Seneca Bridge*
   This strikingly beautiful bridge was built in 1914, and spans the Sandusky River on TR 143.

7. *Abbott's Bridge*
   Water and latrines are available at the far end of the bridge.

8. *1879 Church & Pleasant Union Cemetery*
   Elegant in its simplicity, this white frame country church stands across the road from the ornately fenced Pleasant Union Cemetery. The cemetery is home to a large war memorial to Americans who have died in war from the Revolution to Viet Nam, Gettysburg to Shiloh.

9. *Old Fort, Ohio*
   Although the nearby community of Fort Seneca has the name, the actual site of the now vanished fort was at present day Old Fort, Ohio. As you approach the town on CR 51, keep an eye out for the stone tablet at CR 51 and Harrison Street that marks the spot of William Henry Harrison's 1813 Fort Seneca. It was on this spot that General Harrison received from Commodore Perry the famous message "We have met the enemy and they are ours".

10. *1924 Metal Bridge*

11. *Green Springs, Ohio*
    Home of the "world's largest natural sulphur springs", people would travel great distances to this one-time resort seeking the healing properties of the water. The Seneca Indians also were aware of the unusual properties of the waters, and attempted to choke off the springs when they were forced from the area in 1814. The springs can be found in the idyllic park-like setting of the St. Francis complex on the north edge of town. The park is open daily to the public, and can be entered at the "Medical Building" gate.

12. *Decker Cemetery*
    In this windblown cemetery that stands alone in a farm field just north of TR 173 on CR 53 are buried three veterans of the War of 1812.

13. *Gilmore Bridge*
    The two spans of the Gilmore Bridge over the Sandusky River, while still standing, are no longer open to vehicular traffic.

NOTES/PHOTOS

LOOP #1

SCALE OF MILES

LOOP #2

Length: 45/30 miles

Terrain: Flat to gently rolling

County: Hancock

Down By The Old Mill Stream

This loop, one of two from Van Buren State Park, traverses the open countryside of Hancock County, skirts the eastern fringe of Findlay, then winds along the banks of the Blanchard River before circling northward again through open countryside. Along the way are one room schoolhouses, ornate iron bridges, parks, and beautiful country houses, dotting the landscape through which flows one of the most sung about streams in the world.

A century and a half ago, in the year 1835, Michael Misamore built a mill, the first frame structure in Amanda Township, Hancock County, Ohio, along the banks of the beautiful Blanchard River. The mill was run by water power, which was described in an early history book as "uncertain, through freezing in winter and low water in summer. Nevertheless, it was a great boon to the pioneers of the surrounding country, who often had to travel long distances through forest, with a small grist, ere the little ones could taste the luxury of a wheat cake."

While providing the little ones a taste of a wheat cake was the mill's main purpose, romance proved to be a more lasting product. In 1910, Tell Taylor was inspired to write of the mill on the Blancard River one of the most famous songs of all time, "Down by the Old Mill Stream". Taylor, born on a farm near Vanlue and reared and educated in Findlay, moved to New York in 1897 and, with two other men, opened one of the first publishing houses on Tin Pan Alley. It was on a return visit to Hancock County in 1908 that he wrote the famous song. Taylor returned to Findlay for good in 1922, and is buried in a cemetery near Vanlue, along the river that he loved and made famous. "The old mill wheel is silent, and has fallen down", wrote Taylor, and today there is no trace left at all of the mill. However, the stream that gave rise to the mill and inspired the song is still meandering through the countryside of Hancock County, Ohio, flowing beneath the beautiful bridges of Tell Taylor's day, compelling us to slow our pace, if only for a little while, down by the old mill stream.

For travelers desiring a shorter loop, a 30 mile ride is provided by taking the short cut indicated on the map after your visit to Riverbend Park. Cyclists opting for the shorter loop, however, forfeit the right to sing "Down By The Old Mill Stream" in rounds as they head back into the wind to Van Buren State Park.

Campers are advised that another day of exploring is available with "The Andrews Raiders Ride", also departing from Van Buren State Park.

POINTS OF INTEREST:

1. *Van Buren State Park*
   The ride begins in Van Buren State Park, a small park located east of the railroad tracks and south of TR 218. The park offers camping (no electricity, vault toilets), picnicking, and a shelterhouse.

2. *The Little Red Schoolhouse*
   This charming 1850's schoolhouse, complete with privies and pump, has been restored inside and out by the Hancock County Retired Teachers Association and the Hancock Historical Museum. Hours are by appointment.

3. *The Blanchard River: The Old Mill Stream*
   A winding little road, TR 208, follows the beloved river that is immortalized in Tell Taylor's "Down By The Old Mill Stream". This scenic stretch is only a few miles downstream from the spot of the old mill he described. Ironically, the river was earlier called "Tailor's River" by the Indians after the tailor Blanchard.

4. *Riverbend Park*
   The route passes through Hancock County's Riverbend Park, where drinking water, latrines, and picnic facilities are available.

5. *Reservoir Overlook*
   For travelers feeling the need for a little extra exertion, a hike up the earthen levee of the Findlay Reservoir may provide a glimpse of waterfowl on the man-made lake.

6. *1879 Metal Bridge*
   This beautiful bridge over the Blanchard River on TR 207 was constructed in 1879 by the Columbia Bridge Works of Dayton, Ohio. After crossing the bridge, make a right turn onto TR 244.

7. *1876 Metal Bridge*
   Located just west of the loop on TR 205 is another ornate metal bridge, this one constructed by the Wrought Iron Bridge Company of Canton, Ohio.

8. *One Room Schoolhouse*
   Located just east of the loop on TR 205 is a one room schoolhouse from 1889, used more recently as the Riverside Grange.

9. *Route Note:* Hazardous crossing of SR 15.

10. *Van Horn Cemetery*
    Here, in the center of this little cemetery, nestled between two small shrubs, is the grave marker of Tell Taylor, 1876-1937, that reads "author-composer-publisher, whose inspired song 'Down By The Old Mill Stream' continues to give pleasure to millions and to endear his memory in the hearts of his friends and neighbors of Hancock County". Upon leaving the cemetery, make a right jog to follow TR 190.

11. *Misamore Mill Site*
    Mill stream devotees can stand on the bridge on CR 169 just west of the loop and look north to the east bank where the famed mill once stood along the Blanchard River.

12. *1885 Schoolhouse*
    Here is yet another of the century-old former schoolhouses that dot the countryside of rural Ohio.

13. *Vanlue, Ohio*
    Tell Taylor was born in Vanlue in 1876. Follow SR 330 through the village, north to TR 175.

14. *1888 Enon Valley Presbyterian Church*
    In front of the church is the 100 year old church bell, and the little cemetery beside the church is the resting place of at least two early American veterans. Use extra caution along the one-quarter mile stretch of busy U.S. 224 if visiting the church.

15. *Arcadia Community Park*
    Picnicking areas are available in this community park, located just northwest of SR 12.

NOTES/PHOTOS

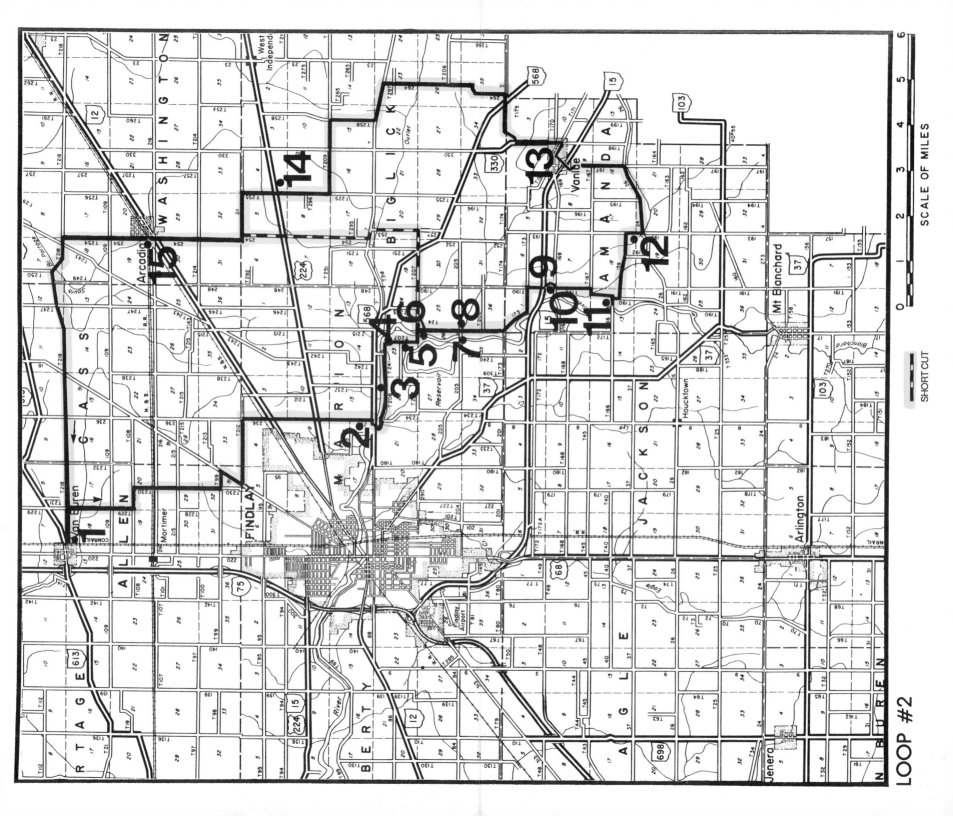

LOOP #2

SCALE OF MILES

SHORT CUT

LOOP #3

Length: 25 miles

Terrain: Flat

County: Hancock

The Andrews Raiders Ride

"God loves Ohio or he would not have given her such a galaxy of heroes to defend the nation in its hour of trial."
— Rutherford B. Hayes
U.S. President 1877-81

Hancock County has been described by cyclists as one giant bikeway, and indeed, the sparsely traveled lanes that stretch between rows of corn and wheat often seem to be ideal bike paths, although they are actually county and township roads. Cyclists and other backroad buffs will delight in traveling through this checkerboard of emerald and gold that is home to productive farms, small towns, and a pride and heritage that runs back to the Civil War. This ride, one of two from Van Buren State Park, takes the traveler back in time to one of the most daring episodes of the entire War Between the States.

Ohio gave the country Generals Grant, Sherman, and Sheridan, and she also gave more of her sons to the Union Army than any other state, a fact that is poignantly visible with a walk through the early cemeteries along this loop. The little metal G.A.R. markers that attend so many gravestones silently attest to the service of more than half of the state's adult male population to the "Grand Army of the Republic". And on a grander scale, a large memorial to one of the most heroic adventures of the entire war can be found on this ride, a statue and historical marker to the famous Andrews Raiders.

On April 12, 1862, at Big Shanty, Georgia, a raid began that was to capture the imagination of the nation and live on in books and movies, including Walt Disney's "The Great Locomotive Chase". Twenty-two soldiers from the North, mostly Ohioans, had penetrated into northern Georgia, intent on stealing a locomotive and then using it to burn bridges behind them as they made a run for the north. When the crew from the Confederate locomotive

"The General" detrained to eat breakfast, the raiders seized the train and took off north, attempting to destroy the confederate supply lines. Pursuit began immediately, and the great chase did not end until 90 miles later, when the locomotive ran out of fuel and the soldiers were forced to abandon the train. All were captured, and eight of the men were executed for the deed at Atlanta in June, 1862. Eight others escaped confinement, and the remaining Raiders were later paroled. All the participants were awarded the Congressional Medal of Honor, the first recipients of this distinguished honor. In 1891, the state of Ohio erected a monument to the Andrews Raiders in the National Cemetery at Chatanooga, the site of the graves of those executed.

Closer to home, travelers along this Hancock County loop can visit the graves of John R. Porter and William Bensinger, two of the Andrews Raiders buried in their home state of Ohio. Porter was one of the men who escaped from confinement, and Bensinger was exchanged to the North almost a year later. Captain Bensinger's Medal of Honor can be seen at the McComb Library as you pass through town. Following your visit to the library, you may want to stop for a picnic lunch at the community park before heading back through the open countryside to Van Buren State Park.

Campers are advised that another day of exploring is available with the "Down By The Old Mill Stream Ride", also departing from Van Buren State Park.

POINTS OF INTEREST:

1. *Van Buren State Park*
   Located just east of the railroad tracks and south of TR 218, this small state park offers no-frills camping, picnicking, and a shelterhouse. Exit the park and follow SR 613 (Market St.) through town.

2. *Van Buren, Ohio*
   You will see a historical marker in the village square describing the history of the town, which was laid out in 1833. It is named for Martin Van Buren, U.S. President from 1837-41.

3. *Thomas Cemetery*
   Located at the northeast corner of CR 203 and TR 134, this little cemetery contains the graves of about a dozen Civil War veterans, and one veteran of the War of 1812.

4. Union Cemetery

Located just west on Main Street (SR 613) from CR 126, McComb's Union Cemetery is home to an impressive memorial to "Our Honored Dead 1861-1865". The likeness of a Civil War soldier faces south from the top of the monument. Located by the monument is a historical marker to the Andrews' Raiders, including William Bensinger and John R. Porter. Bensinger is buried due south of the monument toward the road, and Porter's grave is located about a dozen rows west of Bensinger's.

5. McComb, Ohio

From the cemetery, travel east on SR 613 (Main St.) through the town of McComb, the second largest community in Hancock County. William Bensinger's Congressional Medal of Honor can be seen at the McComb Library, 113 S. Todd St.

6. Cloe Greiner Memorial Park

A historical marker for the village of McComb can be found beside an early crude log structure in the park. Picnicking facilities, water, and latrines are located here, as is a swimming pool (admission charge for the pool). To reach the park, go south on SR 186 to the edge of town. The park is on the east side of the road.

7. Pleasant Hill Cemetery

On the south side of CR 109 east of CR 139 is the Pleasant Hill Cemetery, where the markers of many Civil War veterans, and at least one veteran of the War of 1812, can be found.

8. Route Note

CR 220 into Van Buren is rather busy, so use extra caution. A berm is available for cyclists.

NOTES/PHOTOS

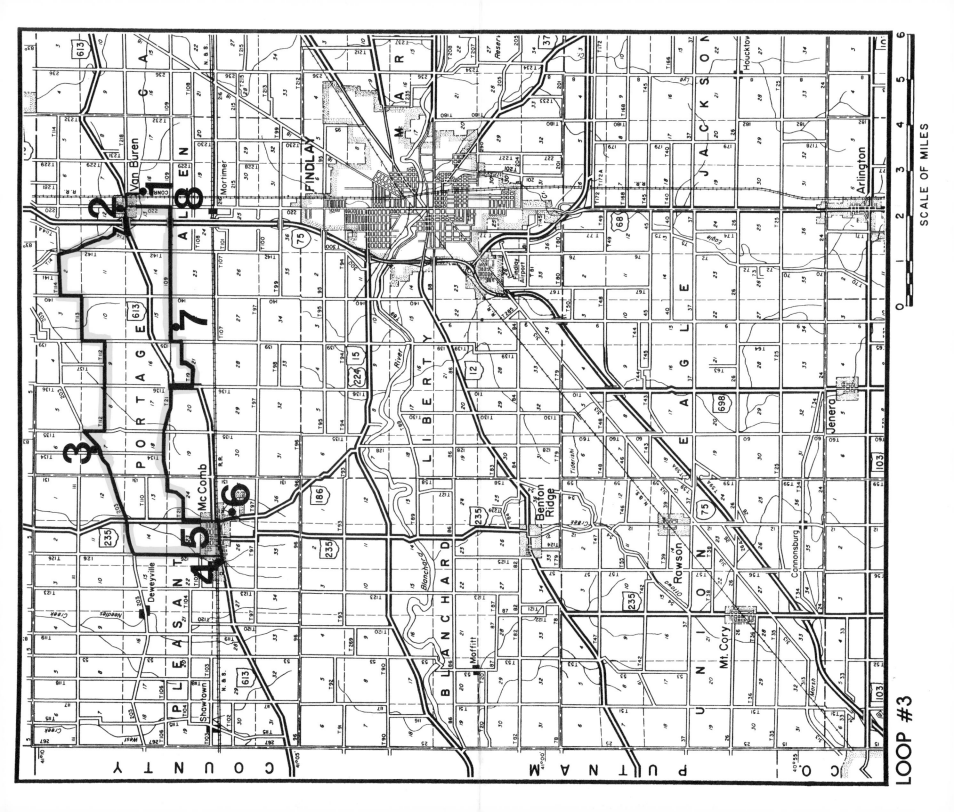

LOOP #3

LOOP #4

Length: 39 miles

Terrain: Mostly flat

County: Ottawa/Lucas

The Crane Creek Ride

Whether your interest is natural history, American history, or simply a riverside ramble through the countryside, this Ottawa County loop, covering 39 miles from the western shore of Lake Erie inland to Genoa, Ohio, offers something for almost every backroad explorer. You may want to begin your trek with an early morning birdwalk through the Magee Marsh, followed by a ride along the Portage River to Elmore, where you can visit the graves of two veterans of the Revolutionary War. After a picnic in a riverside park in Elmore, you'll pass through the town of Genoa, with its shrine, historic outhouse and town hall/opera house, before winding your way to the Ottawa National Wildlife Refuge and an opportunity to see what most Americans have never seen in the wild — the bald eagle. A refreshing swim at the sand beach at Crane Creek finishes off a full day of exploring.

Magee Marsh, a rare example of wild marshland, is known to Ohio birders as the Mecca of Migration, attracting migrating warblers and their watchers every Spring and Fall. Waterfowl are abundant in the preserve, as are other forms of wildlife, including muskrats, foxes, raccoons, and minks. Teeming with life, this treasure along the lake is adjacent to Crane Creek State Park, which offers parking, swimming, and picnic facilities.

Rich not only in natural history, Ottawa County is home to three veterans of the Revolutionary War, and your visit to Elmore will take you to the graves of two of these earliest American veterans, John Green and Israel Harrington. Standing by the simple grave markers of these men, one can feel a connection to the events of Concord and Lexington, Boston and Philadelphia, and imagine the trials and triumphs these men experienced under the command of General George Washington.

From Elmore to Genoa, we shift gears to visit a famous shrine, the Lourdes Grotto, as well as two sites on the National Register of Historic Places, the Town Hall/Opera House and the famous outhouse. The Town Hall was built in 1885, and the Opera House, located on the second floor, was built the following year. The Hall was used not only for theater, but for the yearly caucuses, Medicine Shows, and even a coroner's inquest of the town's first murder. Placed on the National Register of Historic Places in 1976, the Hall earned a place in Chesley's Collection of Historic Theatres in 1983.

Less imposing, but also on the National Register, is the privy on the grounds of the Camper Elementary School, one of the last of its kind. Built in 1870, this elegant brick outhouse, if located away from the school on a country road, could easily be mistaken for a little one-room schoolhouse, as it is built along the same lines.

Near the end of your travels, you'll pass the Ottawa National Wildlife Refuge. In the days when John Green and Israel Harrington were fighting for independence, the bald eagle, our national symbol, was abundant along the shores of Lake Erie. But as their habitat disappeared and pesticides weakened their egg shells, they became an endangered species. By 1975, only four active eagle nests remained in Ohio. The eagle is now making a comeback, and Ottawa Refuge is considered one of the best places in the Midwest to see these raptors. You may wish to stop here for a visit before taking that plunge into Lake Erie at the beach at Crane Creek State Park.

POINTS OF INTEREST:

1. *Crane Creek State Park*
   The ride begins at Crane Creek State Park, where a parking lot, swimming beach, and picnic facilities are available.

2. *Magee Marsh Wildlife Area*
   This superb wildlife area is located adjacent to Crane Creek State Park. Wildlife and birdlife abound along the nature trails that wind along the levees. The trails begin at the beach parking lot. Observation towers and displays are located at the Wildlife Experiment Station on the park road as you leave the park. Hours for the Station are 8-5 M-F, and summer Saturdays 8:30-5, summer Sundays 12-6.

3. *Route Note*
   SR 2, the only road to the refuge, is very busy, and on summer weekends, also carries Cedar Point bound travelers. A narrow berm is available, and the distance is only about one-half mile each way. Nevertheless, persons choosing to travel by bicycle are advised that it is a hazardous road, and extra caution is advised.

4. *Harris-Elmore Union Cemetery*
   John Green, a soldier of the Revolutionary War, is buried in this cemetery. To reach the cemetery, turn south on Schultz-Portage Road. Enter
   the second drive into the cemetery, and you'll find Mr. Green's marker
   by the flag pole, about eight rows south of the drive. Following your
   visit, return to Portage River South Rd.

5. *Harrington Cemetery*
   This very old, well maintained cemetery, surrounded by an iron fence,
   is the last resting place of Israel Harrington, another veteran of the
   Revolutionary War. His marker reads "Pvt., Allen's Vermont Militia, Revolutionary War, died Sept. 10, 1825." Beside his marker is a marker
   to his son and namesake, "Judge, First Trustee, First Minister U.B. Sandusky Circuit, 1830." The cemetery is located on the north side of
   Rice St. (Portage River South Rd.) as you enter Elmore.

6. *Elmore, Ohio*
   For travelers wishing to stop for a picnic, two options are available
   in Elmore. The Walter Ory Park is located just off the loop on the south
   side of Rice St. about two blocks beyond Toledo Street. Picnic tables,
   drinking water, a restored train depot and log house are found in
   the park. A riverside park with picnic tables is available on the loop
   just after your turn onto SR 51 (Toledo St.). To continue on the loop,
   take SR 51 (Toledo St.) over the river to CR 213.

7. *Genoa, Ohio*
   History buffs will delight in a ride down Main Street (CR 51). After
   entering the town, you'll see the fascinating Lourdes Grotto on the
   west side of the street. The famous privy of the Camper Elementary
   School is just north of the Grotto, and Genoa's Town Hall/Opera House
   is on the east side of Main Street in the center of town. At SR 51,
   make a right to Holts East Rd. (T40), then left.

8. *Ottawa National Wildlife Refuge*
   The refuge is open sunrise to sunset, year round. Nature trails are
   provided through the refuge. There is an admission charge of $2.00
   per vehicle, but bicycles are admitted free. However, bicycles are
   not permitted on the trails.

NOTES/PHOTOS

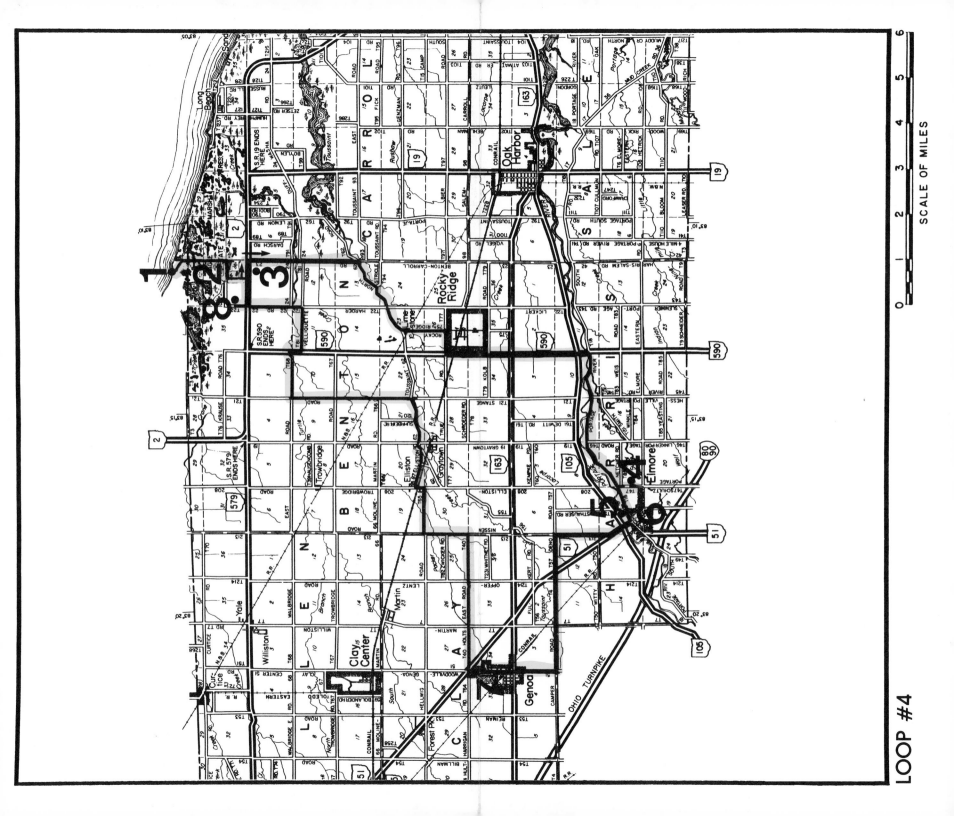

LOOP #4

LOOP #5

Length: 48 miles

Terrain: Flat to rolling, with a few hills

County: Wyandot/Seneca/Hancock

The Tarhe Trek

This lovely ride through the northwest quarter of Wyandot County begins with a visit to the Ice Age, then takes us through two centuries of strife and settlement in Northwest Ohio. Along the way are the signposts of the settlers, the old cemeteries, country churches, one room schoolhouses, a covered bridge, and an old mill. A memorial to a great Indian chief and a marker to a battle between the Indians and the army stand mutely along these backroads, reminding us of the price paid for this soil. Deeds of honor and deeds of horror all took place in this gently rolling countryside, seen from these ridgetops today as a panorama of beautiful farms and farmhouses.

So rich is the Indian history in Wyandot County that the county takes it very name from one of the dominant tribes here in the eighteenth century. Several Indian villages were located along the San-doo-stee River (later mistakenly called "Sandusky"), including Cranetown, home of one of the greatest Indian chiefs in the Ohio Country. Tarhe, the Crane, was behind only Little Turtle and Blue Jacket in command of the Indian forces that amassed to fight the Indian Wars of the 1790's, and these forces defeated the American Army twice before finally falling to General "Mad" Anthony Wayne. And it was Tarhe, chief of the Wyandots, who was given the wampum belt of peace on behalf of the Indian tribes by Anthony Wayne at the signing of the Treaty of Greenville in 1795.

In 1811, in the face of pressure from Tecumseh to join in the great uprising, Tarhe declared that he still held high the "wide white wampum of peace", and would not again wage war against the Americans. Two years later, when the United States was at war with Great Britain and Tecumseh's federation of tribes, William Henry Harrison appealed for help from the neutral tribes. Tarhe responded, "We have been waiting many moons for an invitation to fight for the Americans. I speak on behalf of all the tribes present when I profess our friendship. We have agreed, without any dissension, to join you." Today, along a little country road, the backroad explorer will find a marker, nearly obscured by bushes, that reads simply, "Distinguished Wyandot Chief and Loyal American, Tarhe, died here in Cranetown in 1818".

It was in the same year of Tarhe's passing that the United States government gave 16,000 acres of land here to the Wyandot Indians. The land, being wet and marshy, was unsuitable for agriculture, but was excellent for hunting and trapping. Fed by cool, calcium-rich springs, the marshes supported a wide variety of plant and animal life, with several species dating back to the Ice Age. Now the largest remaining inland wetland in this part of the state, travelers can visit this prehistoric remnant at Springville Marsh and stroll along the boardwalk observing nature's bounty.

One other event commemorated the loyalty of the Wyandots during the War of 1812, the giving of Indian Mill to the Indians for their use in grinding wheat into flour. Near the site of that mill is the Indian Mill State Memorial, the nation's first museum of milling in an original mill. You can tour the mill, then take a refreshing break across the river at a scenic park and picnic spot, which is also the ideal location for taking photographs of the picturesque old mill.

POINTS OF INTEREST:

1. *Carey, Ohio*
   The ride begins near Carey, and bicyclists may want to park in the village and travel SR 199 north to T5 to join the loop. As always, extra caution is advised along state routes. A narrow berm is available for cyclists along SR 199. Food and drink are available in the town.

2. *Springville Marsh State Nature Preserve*
   Located on the south side of T24, visitors can stroll through the marsh on a boardwalk, and use the observation tower to spot the wildlife that abounds here.

3. *1878 German Baptist Church*
   Now the Oak Grove Church of the Brethren, this country church was built more than a century ago by German settlers. It is located on the southwest corner of T206 and T266.

4. *Lutheran Ridge Cemetery*
   This early cemetery straddles T95 just inside Wyandot County. Stones dating back to at least 1839 can be found here, as can several

markers bearing interesting inscriptions and artwork. One marker, from 1864, testifies that the man was a member of the Ohio National Guard.

5. *Caution: Hazardous Crossing of SR 15*

6. *1894 Schoolhouse*
   This abandoned one-room schoolhouse at C96 and T42 is unusual in that it still boasts the old bell tower, sans bell, that would summon the children to class from the surrounding countryside.

7. *St. Joseph's Catholic Church*
   This magnificent brick country church looms above the fields as you approach it along C103.

8. *North Salem Lutheran Church*
   This church, altered in 1972, was originally built in 1850. A walk through the adjacent cemetery reveals a number of early markers, including many written in German.

9. *Caution: Hazardous Crossing of SR 23*

10. *Colonel Crawford Monument*
    Located at the intersection of SR 67 and C47 is a marker commemorating the defeat of Colonel William Crawford at Battle Island in 1782. It was here that the Indians wreaked a terrible vengeance on Crawford for the earlier massacre of the Moravian Indians at Gnadenhutten. Crawford was not responsible for the massacre, but his associate, David Williamson, who fled, was. The torture that the tribes had planned for Williamson was exacted on Crawford in his place. Although called Battle Island, the battle took place here, and not on an island.

11. *Indian Mill*
    Located by a large metal bridge where C47 crosses the Sandusky River, the mill is now a museum of milling, operated by the Ohio Historical Society. Hours of operation are Thurs 1-5, Fri-Sat 9:30-5, Sun 1-6, June through October. Adults $1.00, students .50. Across the river from the mill is a park and picnic area with restrooms, and a display of the millstones used by the Wyandots before Indian Mill was constructed.

12. *Parker Covered Bridge*
    Built in 1873 by J.C. Davis, this Howe Truss covered bridge spans the Sandusky River on T40. It is one of only two covered bridges still in use in the county.

13. *Tarhe Monument*
    Located left about one-half mile on C37, travelers can visit this modest memorial to the great Wyandot chief.

14. *Caution: Route Note*
    Use extra caution as you travel this short stretch of SR 53. A narrow berm is available for cyclists.

15. *Cemetery*
    An early cemetery can be found just beyond the turn from 105 to T11.

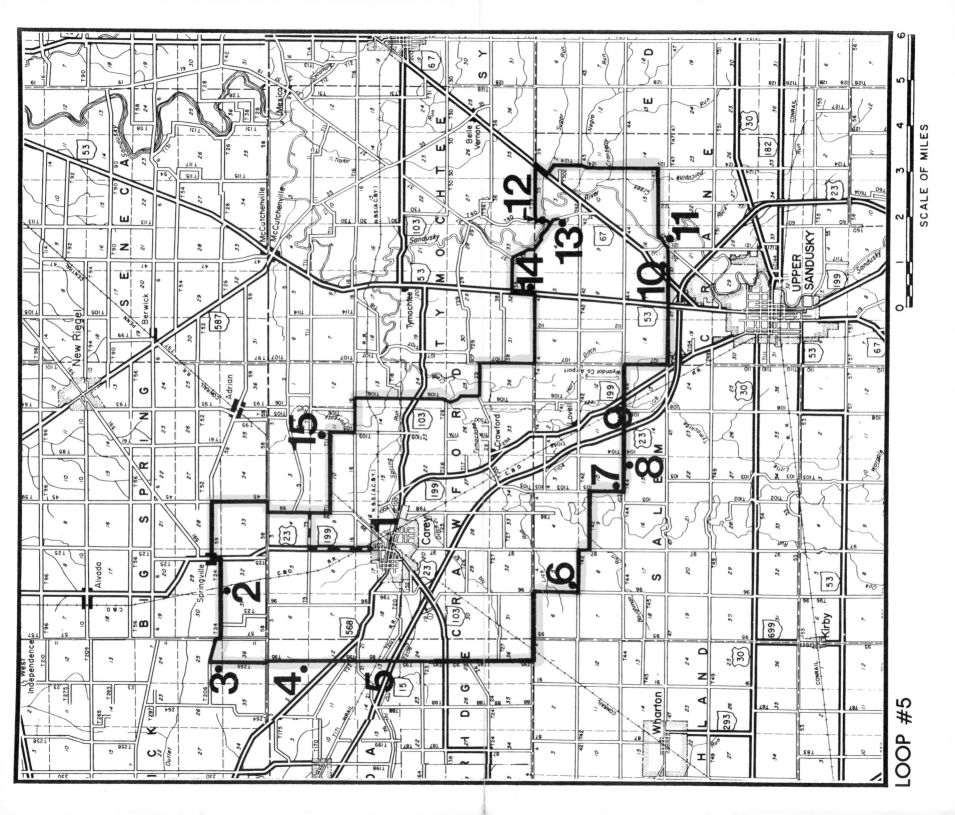

LOOP #5

SCALE OF MILES

LOOP #6

Length: 48 miles

Terrain: Flat

County: Defiance/Henry/Fulton

The Black Swamp Ride

This country ride over the rich, flat farmland of northwest Ohio begins along the banks of the beautiful Maumee River, then crosses open countryside on a journey back in time, passing through a time tunnel of trees before re-emerging to curve gently along country roads past beautiful red barns, one room schoolhouses, and country churches. "It is an interesting country to travel through", wrote historian Henry Howe in 1849. And nearly a century and a half later, it remains so.

"A greater part of this country is covered by the famous Black Swamp, sustaining a magnificent forest almost impenetrable to the rays of the sun", wrote Howe. While the pioneers virtually wiped out the great forest, travelers along this loop today can look back in time and see a rare reminder of this magnificent woodland at Goll Woods, an essentially virgin woodlot that survived the ages thanks to the Goll family's love of their "Big Woods". Peter Goll, Sr., his wife Catherine, and son Peter Jr. came from Dobs, France in 1836. They were farmers, but they also loved the trees, and for four generations the Goll family resisted the efforts of the timber operators. In 1966 the land was acquired by the State of Ohio as the last remnant of primeval forest in northwest Ohio. Trees dating back more than five centuries still live here, stretching their branches to the sky more than one-hundred feet above the woodland floor. In spring, a carpet of wildflowers races to blossom before the budding leaves above shut out the sunshine until winter; in summer, the traveler will find respite from the heat of the surrounding countryside in this island of trees; and in fall, the magnificence of the woods is unsurpassed.

The Great Black Swamp, a Connecticut-sized legacy of an earlier and larger Lake Erie, slowed settlement in northwest Ohio, but an undertaking of Herculean proportions conquered the swamp and brought settlers and agriculture to the region. The markers of this triumph, considered one of the greatest such efforts in the world, attract virtually no attention from the traveler rushing by them today, but the huge roadside ditches along these country roads are indeed historic. More than 125 years ago, industrious German pioneer families began digging ditches to drain the swamp, and our friend Howe noted prophetically at the time that "probably, in less than a century, when it shall be cleared and drained, it will be the garden of Ohio, and support half a million people". When the area was drained, land values shot up from $2.00 per acre to $10.00 per acre, and today, while the area accounts for only 11% of the state's land, it provides 25% of the state's agricultural income.

While the roadside ditches were used to carry water away from the fields, another ditch was being dug at about the same time to bring water through the area. The Miami and Erie Canal, called by many the "Big Ditch", connected the Ohio River and Lake Erie, providing access to the larger markets for the farmers of the region. A six mile long stretch of the old canal still survives along the Maumee River at Independence Dam State Park, and hikers can walk along the old towpath where the mules trod over a century ago. With the old canal, the big woods, and the scattering of old schoolhouses and churches, this area truly remains "an interesting country to travel through".

POINTS OF INTEREST:

1. *Independence Dam State Park*
   Located off SR 424 between the Maumee River and the Miami and Erie Canal, this beautiful park offers hiking trails along the old towpath, picnic facilities, and camping (no electricity, vault toilets). Three miles of riverside riding are available in the park, and a historical marker at the entrance to the park provides information about the old canal.

2. *Route Note*
   Travelers are reminded to use extra caution when traveling along or crossing state routes, such as SR 24.

3. *1899 Schoolhouse*
   Like all the old schoolhouses along the loop, this one room brick schoolhouse is located on private property but is clearly in view from the road.

4. *St. Markus Kirche*
   This beautiful brick country church, built by the descendants of the German pioneer families in the area, dates back to 1895.

5. *1894 Schoolhouse*

6. *Goll Woods State Nature Preserve*
   Visitors to this beautiful primeval woodland are reminded to "take only photographs and leave only footprints". Trails are available, as is parking and restroom facilities. The entrance is located along TR 26.

7. *Goll Cemetery*
   Located just west of the loop on TR F is the historic Goll Cemetery, where the generations of the Golls are buried. It is due to their foresightedness that we are able to enjoy this last remaining remnant of the great Ohio forest in this part of the state.

8. *1883 Schoolhouse*

9. *1876 Schoolhouse*

10. *Route Note*
    There is a one-quarter mile stretch of gravel road between SR 34 and SR 66.

11. *Bethlehem Lutheran Church*
    Located along the curve in Adams Ridge Rd. is this charming brick country church. The date plate, however, is broken and illegible.

12. *Cemetery*
    This little cemetery is unusual due to the arrangement of stones in a semi-circle at the rear of the cemetery.

NOTES/PHOTOS

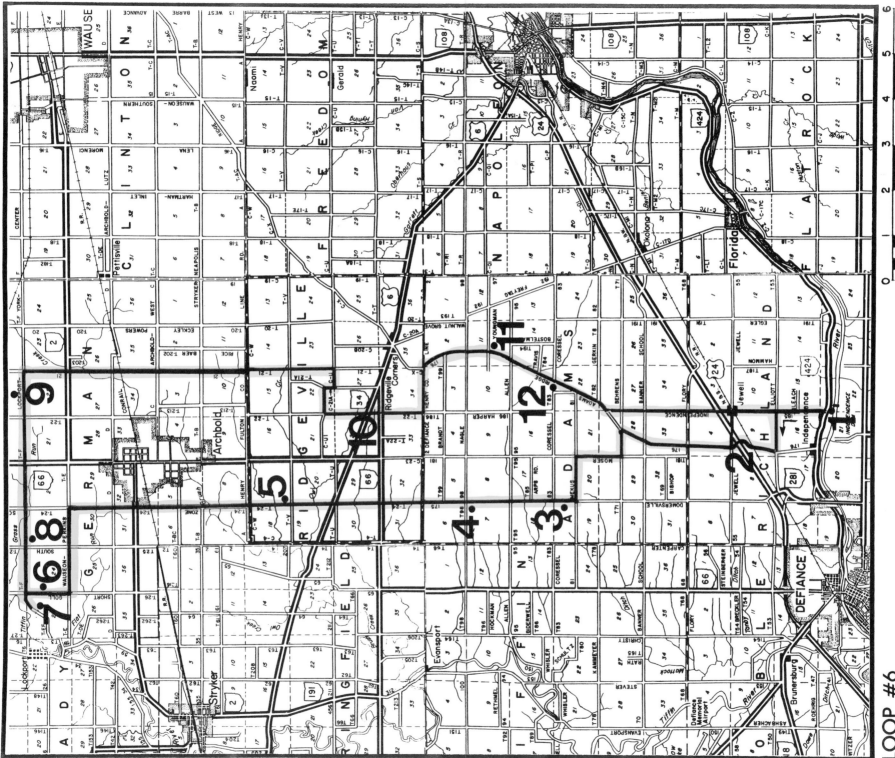

LOOP #6

SCALE OF MILES

LOOP #7

Length: 47/31 miles

Terrain: Flat to rolling

County: Fulton/Williams

The Great Northwest Ride

This enchanting ride through the northwest corner of Ohio takes the traveler from Harrison Lake State Park through the country-side of Williams County, stretching over the gently rolling terrain to visit prehistoric Indian mounds in Ohio's most northwesterly township. Along the way are century old country churches and peaceful pioneer cemeteries, nestled in valleys that are home to beautiful barns and rolling green pastures, lakes that offer rest to wildlife and wanderer alike, and a historic log cabin that sits on a hill looking over the fertile fields around it.

Traveling through an area of open countryside, it's easy to imagine that what we see is all there ever was, with the exception of perhaps a few trees. But the land is like a chalkboard, having been written upon and erased, time after time. Empty crossroads may have been towns, and fields of corn may grow over old battlefields. Only rarely does the eraser of time miss its mark, and leave a covered bridge, an old mill, a one-room schoolhouse, or perhaps a log cabin, protruding above the sands of time for even a century. How extraordinary it is indeed when a signpost of a civilization that thrived here 2,000 years ago remains for today's explorer to visit, casting the imagination back to that long ago time.

Two millenia ago, an elaborate and artistic society was centered in the Ohio Valley, a society that we today call the Hopewell. Living chiefly in riverside towns, the people of this society built great burial mounds and earthworks, and carried on trading from the Rockies to the Atlantic. The mounds left behind by this vanished society were cause for great, and often wild, speculation by the first settlers who came into Ohio. The Indians living here at the time were equally puzzled as to who built the mysterious mounds. It is unusual to find the remnants of the Hopewell Culture this far north in Ohio, but the four inauspicious mounds of earth along Nettle Creek in Williams County give testimony that the Hopewells were indeed here.

After visiting the mounds at Nettle Creek, a rest awaits you at beautiful Lake La Su An before you journey on through Pioneer, Ohio and back to Harrison Lake. A refreshing swim at the beach awaits you at journey's end. For persons wishing not to travel so far back in time, a short cut is provided on the map after your visit to the restored log cabin and metal bridge.

Campers are advised that another day of exploring is available with "The Winameg Wander", a loop that also departs from Harrison Lake.

POINTS OF INTEREST:

1. *Harrison Lake State Park*
   Class A (electricity and showers) and B (no electric, latrines) camping is available at this state park, as well as swimming and picnicking.

2. *1875 Church*

3. *Jacob Young Log House*

4. *1909 Metal Bridge*

5. *Church Bell and Old Millstone*
   Located at SR 576 and P-50, the 1892 bell sits in front of the old church. On the same corner is an old millstone with a historical marker indicating that the stone was first used in a mill built in 1844, and later used in a mill in 1852 that was located one half mile east of this spot.

6. *Nettle Lake Indian Mounds*
   The drive that leads back to the mounds is easy to miss, especially when the corn is up. It is located precisely one-half mile north of road R on the east side of road 4.75. Historical markers describe the history of the mounds and the Hopewells.

7. *Nettle Lake U.B. Church and Cemetery*
   Veterans of the Civil War and the War of 1812 are buried in this peaceful little cemetery across from the old church.

8. *Lake La Su An*
   This beautiful wildlife area is operated by the Ohio Department of Natural Resources as a hunting and fishing preserve.

9. *North Bridgewater Church*
Located at SR 576 and R, this picturesque church is more ornate than many of its type.

10. *Pioneer, Ohio*
As you pass through the center of this quaint village, you will make a slight left jog at the traffic light.

A Note to the Navigator: Williams County uses a simple grid system in numbering their roads. East-west roads are lettered, south-north roads are numbered, consecutively, at one mile intervals. Roads located between the intervals use decimals, e.g. P-50 is an east-west road halfway between P and Q; 4.75 is a north-south road located three-fourths of the way between roads 4 and 5. Because the county has chosen to use two different systems for their maps and road signage, a grid has been added as a key for identifying all roads in the county. Each road along this loop is identified in parentheses at each turn. Simply use the parentheses and the grid in identifying the roads in Williams County.

NOTES/PHOTOS

SHORT LOOP

SCALE OF MILES

FULTON CO.

LOOP #7

N

LOOP #8

Length: 42 miles

Terrain: Flat to rolling

County: Fulton

The Winameg Wander

This 42 mile meander over the gently rolling terrain of Fulton County takes the rider from Harrison Lake to one of the most famous trees in Ohio history, the Great Council Oak at Winameg. Log houses, pioneer cemeteries, and the last remaining old country store in the county are added features of this serene, and somewhat sandy, sojourn. Our traveler will retrace the route of the early explorers who traveled these same sand ridges, known as the Oak Openings, through the now vanished Great Black Swamp of northwest Ohio.

A little more than a century ago, this land was drained and the swamp forest virtually eliminated. While the trees of Ohio's forests for the most part vanished anonymously, a few others live on, not only in life, but in history and legend. If Ohio had a Hall of Fame for trees, it would undoubtedly include such notables as the Whispering Oak of Preble County, the Three Sisters of Greene County, the late Logan Elm of Pickaway County, and the star of this loop, the 500 year old Council Oak of Fulton County. Some trees have gained enduring fame for their own stature and longevity, while others have become treasures because of the human events they have witnessed. In Ohio, the events of note are usually connected with Indian and white relations, and that is the case with the Council Oak, a tree that cast its shade over peace talks and held prisoners fast to its trunk for torture.

Two men epitomized the delicate relations of the Indians and whites in the 1830's, and these two men, Chief Winameg and Colonel D.W.H. Howard, are buried almost side by side beneath the towering tree that saw terror and tribute. Col. Howard was appointed Indian interpreter by President Andrew Jackson, and often held councils under the tree that stood by his home in Winameg, a town that took its name from the Indian village of the Potawotamies. In 1832, at the time of the Black Hawk War, Col. Howard held a council under the tree that was credited with doing more to prevent Indian War than any other man in northwest Ohio.

Chief Winameg, the aged sachem of the Potawotamies who lived in the Indian village bearing his name, had seen 100 winters when he was first introduced to Col. Howard. Winameg and Howard had a deep personal respect for one another, and this respect was shown in the words of Col. Howard: "I was an interpreter at a Council held under the Council Oak by the aged Chief Winameg, who lies buried in the hill. At the foot of the Great Council Oak the Indian Council fire burned out, and he sleeps his last sleep in the hill by the spring. And may I, too, when the drum beats the last roll call, be permitted to pitch Eternity's Bivouac on the hillside, in the shade of the beautiful tree. So may it be." And so it is that travelers along the winding little road that passes through Winameg, Ohio can see along the banks of a little creek the giant oak that casts its shadow over the graves of two great men, Chief Winameg and Colonel D.W.H. Howard.

More than a century and a half has passed since that council. Today, Winameg remains a sleepy hamlet, home to an old general store that dates back to the Civil War, a cemetery that is home to the children of Col. Howard and the successor of Winameg, Chief Wyoxie. A historical marker stands in front of the beautiful white house on the hill that was home to Howard, and a simple sign reading "Council Oak" tilts in front of the towering old oak by the banks of Bad Creek.

Following your visit to Winameg, you'll return to more sand at Harrison Lake, where a swim at the beach awaits you. Campers are advised that another day of exploring is available with "The Great Northwest Ride", also departing from Harrison Lake.

POINTS OF INTEREST:

1. *Harrison Lake State Park*
   Class A (electricity, entrance on west side) and Class B (no electricity, entrance on east side) camping is available, as well as swimming and picnicking.

2. *Fayette, Ohio*
   Travelers passing through the little village on the first Saturday of August will see trucks adorned with thistles, floats acclaiming thistles, and a thistle-growing competition at the city park. Chicken BBQ and homemade pies complete the festivities of the "Bull Thistle Parade", a tribute and surrender to the stubborn weeds that grow in the fields.

3. *Route Note*

The road becomes gravel for a short stretch of about one-half mile between Bean Creek and SR 108.

4. *The Giant Coffee Pot*

Travelers may notice a huge coffee pot up on a pole as they pass by this private residence. It is actually a pigeon house, inspired by the water tower (sans handle and spout) at West Unity.

5. *Aetna Cemetery*

Located on Road 10-2 one-half mile north of Winameg, this old cemetery is the final resting place of the children of D.W.H. Howard, and of Chief Wyoxie, the last successor of Chief Winameg. Chief Wyoxie, one of the few remaining Indians left in the area after their westward removal, was buried here in 1840. No nails were used in his coffin so that he could continue his journey to the afterlife without difficulty. No marker marks the spot.

6. *Winameg, Ohio*

As the traveler enters this little hamlet, a stop at the old country store is of interest. Built in 1865, the old store is probably the last one of its kind still in business in Fulton County.

7. *The Great Council Oak*

The historic tree stands along the bank of Bad Creek just south of the village, and a historical marker describes the history of the famous tree.

8. *Old State Line Road*

This road derives its name from the old state line dispute with Michigan, which unsuccessfully claimed all the northern townships of the border counties of Ohio in the early 1800's.

9. *Metal Bridges*

While crossing only one of the bridges, three of the old steel bridges are in view as you travel these backroads across Bean Creek.

NOTES/PHOTOS

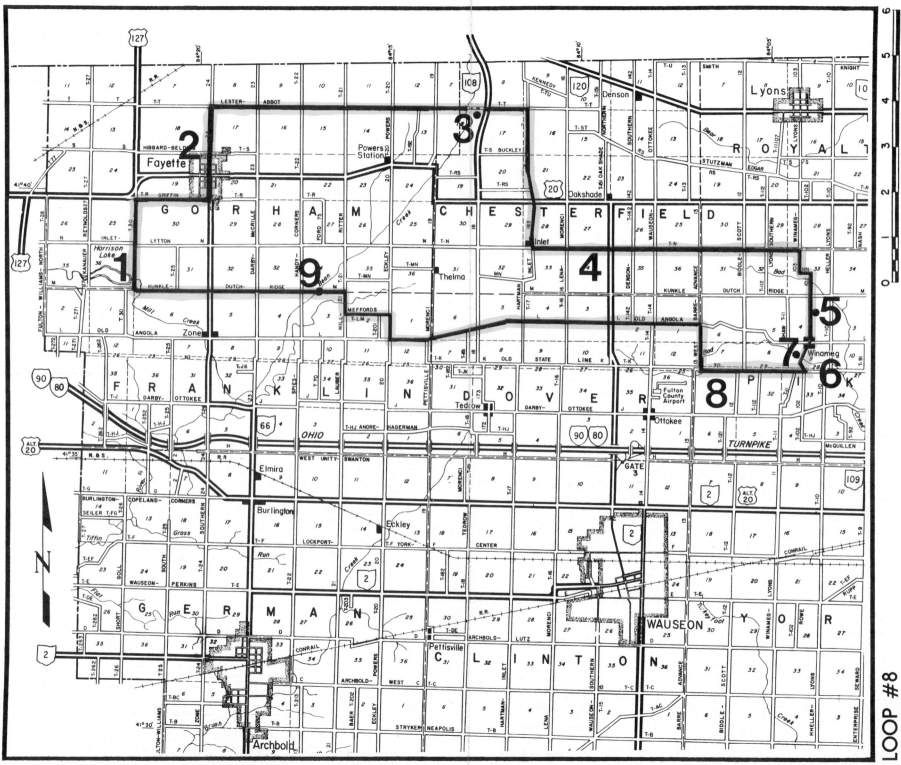

LOOP #8

LOOP #9

Length: 14 miles

Terrain: Flat to gently rolling

County: Erie

Island of Stone

Islands and intrigue seem to go hand in hand, and this sojourn to a place apart can only be described as enchanting. You will ride along the rocky shores of the largest American island in Lake Erie, looking out over the sparkling blue waters, the music of the waves accompanying you as you pedal past Ice Age wonders, Indian mysteries, and the magnificent stone mansions of Kelleys Island.

The story of Kelleys Island is literally written in the rocks, and our island explorer will be able to trace 25,000 years of history in the beautiful limestone of the island. The earliest chapter of the story was written during the Ice Age by the awesome power of a glacier. Far to the north in Canada, snow and ice began piling up, ultimately reaching a height of 8,000 feet. Like putty, the weight of this mass forced the edge to begin spreading out, and as it crept across the landscape, it filled in valleys and rounded off hilltops. On Kelleys Island, the power and artistry of the glacier can be seen in the 400 foot long grooves scoured into the limestone as the glacier's icy edge passed. The world famous Glacial Grooves of Kelleys Island have been a wonder to visitors for over a century.

Mother Nature is not the only writer in rock to have left a legacy on the island. More than three hundred years ago, the Erie Indians, or People of the Panther, lived here. In 1655, a fierce and feared confederation called the Five Nations swept through here like a terrible storm, vanquishing and eliminating the Cat Nation. All that remains of these people on the island today are mysterious, and nearly obliterated, pictographs carved into the smooth surface of Inscription Rock, a large boulder that juts into the water on the south side of the island.

While the glacier and the Indians carved their stories into the rocks, another island author wrote his story with the rocks themselves. Nicholas Smith emigrated from Bavaria in 1858, coming to

Kelleys Island around 1860. Smith was a stone mason, and when this skilled artisan took the beautiful and prized Kelleys Island limestone in hand, the results were many of the beautiful stone buildings that dot the island and delight passersby. Mr. Smith continued to work with stone until he was 80 years old, when he turned to grape growing. Century old stone churches, schools, wine cellars and houses are the monuments to the stone mason's craft standing yet today on Kelleys Island.

With the glacial grooves, Inscription Rock, abandoned quarries and beautiful buildings, a trip to Kelleys Island is a trip to a fascinating gallery of stone.

POINTS OF INTEREST:

1. *Neuman Ferry Dock, Marblehead, Ohio*
This Island adventure begins with a 30 minute ferry ride to the island from the dock at the foot of Francis St. in Marblehead. At this writing, the ferry departs Marblehead just before the half hour, and departs the island on the hour. Parking is available near the dock to leave your car, if so desired. The cost is about $9.00 round trip for an adult with a bicycle. Contact the carrier at (419) 626-5557 to confirm the schedule and prices.

2. *Ferry Dock, Kelleys Island*
To begin your explorations, turn left after leaving the dock.

3. *West Bay Quarry Dock*
The hulking structure that looms ahead of you as you ride around the west side of the island is the old quarry dock, long out of service.

4. *Abandoned Quarries*
On the east side of the road across from the quarry dock are the old stone quarries. Limestone for the first American lock at the Soo was quarried from Kelleys Island, as were the stone border markers for the Indiana-Ohio state line. The occasional hiker and fossil hunter has replaced the quarrymen in the abandoned quarry.

5. *Glacial Grooves*
Considered the most spectacular glacial grooves in the world, this famous site is now under the auspices of the Ohio Historical Society.

6. *Kelleys Island State Park*
A public beach and camping facilities are available at this state park.

7. Kelleys Island Cemetery

In the north end of the cemetery are buried the island's proprietor, Datus Kelley, and his family, including Charles Carpenter, son-in-law and the island's first vintner, and Addison, Datus' son and first resident of the Kelley Mansion. Local legend has it that John McDonald was working on preparing the cemetery, and when accused of poor work habits, replied that he would not ever be buried in the cemetery, so he didn't care. Shortly afterwards, he met an untimely end in the quarry where he worked, and in 1854, became the very first person buried in the cemetery. His grave is in the far northwest corner.

8. Estes School

Built in 1901 using funds given by James Estes, the school is now famous for its one-member graduating classes.

9. North Bay Scenic Spur

This dead-end road follows the scenic rocky shore of the island's North Bay.

10. 1865 Home of Nicholas Smith

This was the home of Nicholas Smith, the stone mason, and his wife. It is now the tasting room of the resurrected Kelleys Island Wine Co.

11. Kelley Mansion

Built for Addison Kelley during the Civil War years of 1861-65, the mansion is on the National Register of Historic Places. Presidents Taft and McKinley have stayed here. The most famous feature of the mansion is the circular staircase in the main hall, built from a single piece of wood. The mansion is open daily for tours. Admission fee.

12. Inscription Rock

Henry Schoolcraft, historian and Indian agent, said of Inscription Rock in the early 19th century, "It is by far the most extensive and well sculptured and best preserved inscription of the antiquarian period ever found in America." The rock has suffered the elements, and is now nearly obliterated. It is a site of the Ohio Historical Society.

13. South Shore Scenic Spur

Civil War era stone houses look out over the blue waters along this scenic spur. Turning around is advised where the road turns north and becomes gravel.

14. Kelley Hall

This Town Hall was a gift to the community from Datus Kelley in 1860. It has seen a variety of uses, ranging from the first high school to church services to a library.

15. *South Side School*

Located in the "downtown" section of the island on the west side of Division Street, this 1853 stone school building is now a rooming house.

16. *Old Stone Church*

This picturesque stone church was built by the German speaking German Reformed Church in 1867. Its last service was the burial of a life-long member in 1942. It is now home to the Kelleys Island Historical Association.

17. *Winery Ruins*

Barely visible through the foliage, the castle-like ruins of the old winery are on private property. The wine industry of Kelleys Island began in the mid-1850's, and of the sparkling Catawba wine it was said that "having once tasted for medicinal purposes only, a Rechabite in temperance in a season of despondency would be sorely tempted for a revivification merely to yield his willing lips".

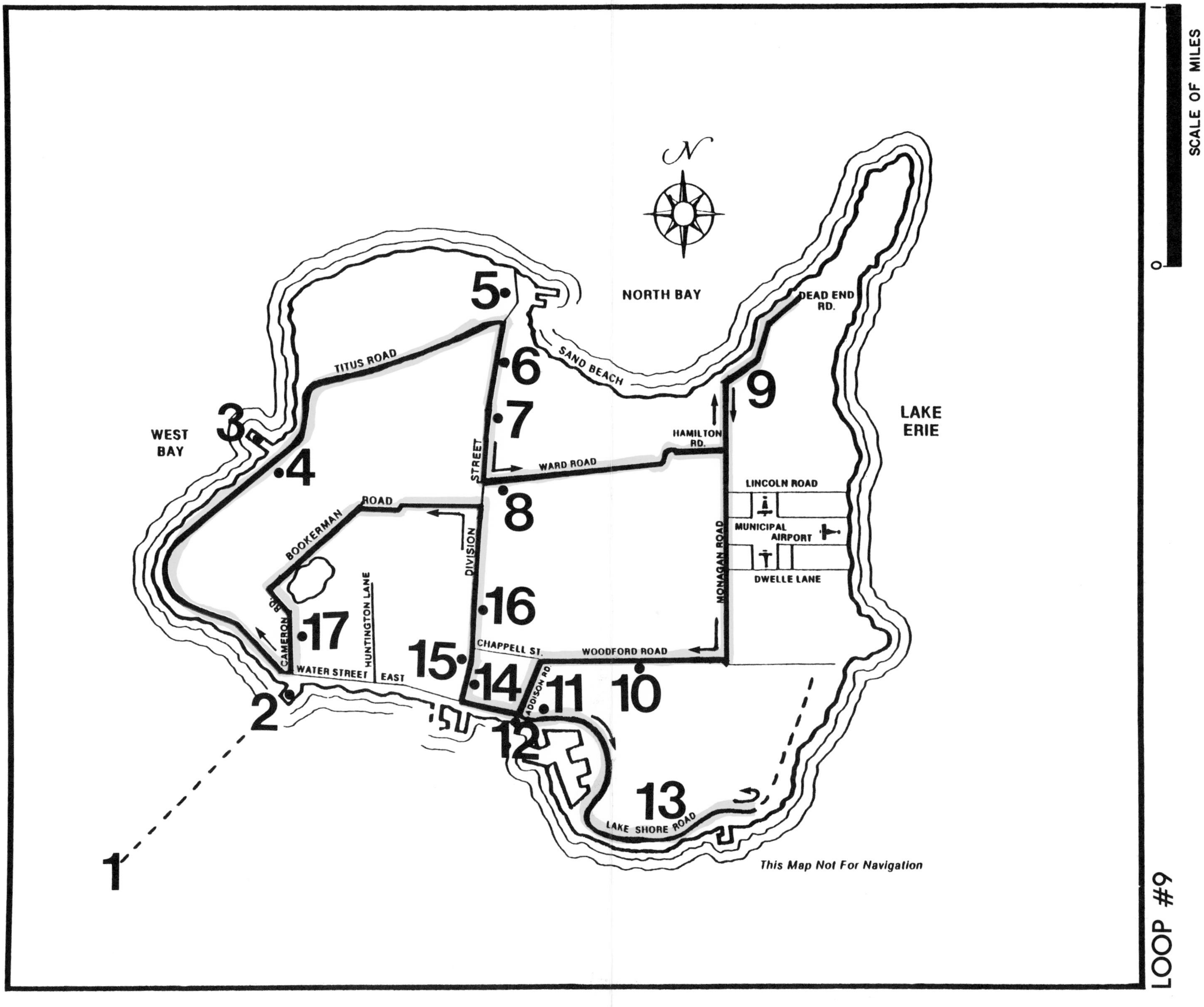

SCALE OF MILES
1
0
N
NORTH BAY
WEST BAY
LAKE ERIE
TITUS ROAD
SAND BEACH
DEAD END RD.
HAMILTON RD.
WARD ROAD
STREET
DIVISION
ROAD
BOOKERMAN
LINCOLN ROAD
MUNICIPAL AIRPORT
DWELLE LANE
MONAGAN ROAD
CAMERON RD.
HUNTINGTON LANE
CHAPPELL ST.
WOODFORD ROAD
WATER STREET EAST
ADDISON RD
LAKE SHORE ROAD
1
2
3
4
5
6
7
8
9
10
11
12
13
14
15
16
17
This Map Not For Navigation

LOOP #9

LOOP #10

Length: 45 miles

Terrain: Gently rolling

County: Mercer

The Road to Recovery

This 45 mile ride over the gently rolling terrain of Mercer County will take you past the fields and meadows of the dairy farms that form the agricultural patchwork of this region. Bovines grazing on the slopes beneath the spires of the tall country churches create a pastoral scene where you will find abandoned one-room schoolhouses, metal bridges, old cemeteries, and one of the most sacred memorials to the men who first ventured into the wilderness of the Ohio Country.

It was just before sunrise on the snowy morning of November 4, 1791. Sent by President Washington to still the Indian attacks along the frontier, the army of General Arthur St. Clair had en-camped on the banks of the Wabash River. Suddenly, out of the stillness of early morning came the war whoops of the Indian forces led by Blue Jacket, Little Turtle, and Simon Girty. The unpre-pared soldiers were completely overwhelmed, and 631 men gave their lives that day. Two years later, General Anthony Wayne, called by the Indians the "American general who never sleeps", returned to the site of the defeat and built Fort Recovery. On June 30, 1794, one of the largest Indian forces ever to engage the American Army attacked the fort. On the site of previous disaster, the forces of General Wayne prevailed, delivering a defeat to the Indians that broke their spirit. Two months later, the war was over with Wayne's victory at Fallen Timbers. So important were these events at Fort Recovery that the Congress erected a memorial that stands today on the square in Fort Recovery, Ohio. The 93 foot high granite shaft entombs the fallen heroes "who, as advance guards, entered the wilderness of the west to blaze the way for freedom and civilization".

After visiting the memorial and the partially reconstructed fort, you'll follow the Greenville Treaty Line out of town and into the beautiful countryside of "The Land of the Cross-Tipped Churches". Picturesque churches dating back nearly a century, tall steeples reaching to the skies, ring the horizon as you ride slowly through this scenic panorama of western Ohio. The names of the small towns and roads along the route bear witness to the importance of the church to these rural communities, names such as St. Rose, St. Wendelin, St. Sebastian, St. Henry, and many more. Biblical names abound on the maps and road signs. The close reader of the map will notice that even the county map maker got caught up in the spirit by identifying our road toward Minster as "Fort Recovery-Minster" Rd.

POINTS OF INTEREST:

1. Grand Lake St. Mary's
The ride begins at the western end of the lake at the picnic grounds, just south of the east terminus of Monroe Road. Grand Lake, built to feed the canal system, was dug from a swamp by 1,700 men who worked for $0.30 a day plus a jigger of whiskey. At the time it was completed, it was the largest man-made lake in the world.

2. Route Note
Bicyclists depart from the roadway to take the Celina-Coldwater Bikeway to Coldwater. At the end of the bikeway in Coldwater, turn right on Vine to SR 118, then south through town. Motorists may follow the marked roads on the map to reach Coldwater.

3. St. Peter Church
Built in 1904, this is but one of the many cross-tipped churches that loom over the landscape of Mercer County.

4. 1890 Metal Bridge
You will cross this old metal bridge over the Wabash River, constructed by the Variety Bridge Co., after turning south onto First St. from Wabash Rd. just inside the Fort Recovery city limit.

5. Fort Recovery Memorial
Located at First St. and Boundary in the town square, this monument was erected in 1912 by Act of Congress.

6. Fort Recovery Historical Site and Museum
Two reconstructed blockhouses and a connecting stockade are found at this Ohio Historical Society site. The museum located here is open May through September, Tues-Sat 1-5, Sun 12-5. Admission charge for museum. The site is located west of the square on Boundary St.

7. *Greenville Treaty Line*
Following Anthony Wayne's victory at Fallen Timbers, the Treaty of Greene Ville was signed in 1795. The Indians conceded land south of the line to settlement, while retaining use of land to the north of the line. Boundary Road follows the line east out of town, where it becomes Ft. Recovery-Minster Rd.

8. *One Room Schoolhouse*
This quaint one room schoolhouse, long out of service and on private property, was built in 1900.

9. *St. Wendelin Church*

10. *1905 St. Francisci Church*

11. *Steepleview Stretch*
This stretch of Homan Road is noted for the number of steeples that can be seen from this vantage point.

12. *St. Sebastian Church*

13. *Route Note: Caution*
Use extra caution along this half-mile stretch of U.S. 127. The road is very busy, but there is a berm available.

14. *The Big Chicken*
In front of the Heyne's egg farm stands the Big Chicken, and an interesting painting on the barn portrays another chicken. The farm even has drive-thru egg pickup.

15. *Route Note*
Cyclists can again pick up the bikeway on St. Anthony Road. Motorists can follow the map back to the picnic grounds at Grand Lake St. Marys.

NOTES/PHOTOS

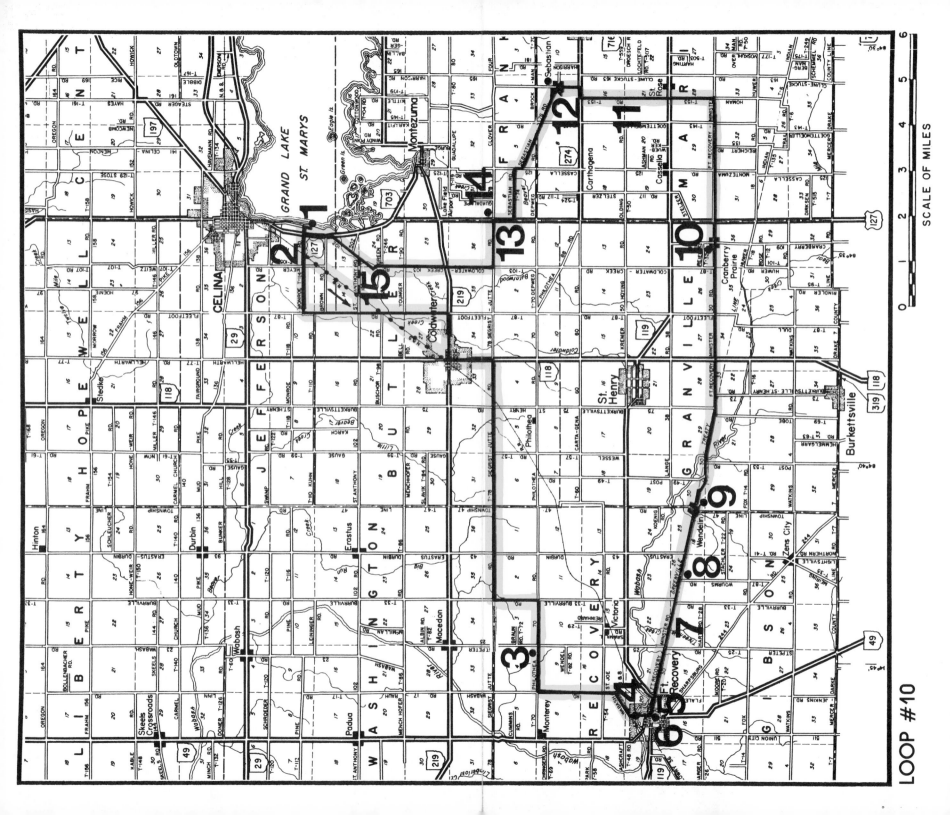

LOOP #10

SCALE OF MILES

LOOP #11

Length: 34 miles

Terrain: Gently rolling

County: Wyandot/Crawford

A Savanna Sojourn

This 34 mile ride over the gently rolling terrain of beautiful Wyandot and Crawford Counties takes the traveler back in time to view the landscape that greeted the early settlers upon their arrival in southwest Crawford County. Along the way are covered and metal bridges, pioneer cemeteries, one-room schoolhouses, and the woods where Frank, the War Horse, is buried. With the pleasing panorama of farms and fields, rivers and streams, this is an outing that today's explorer will certainly enjoy.

The Ohio of two hundred years ago is often thought of as dense forest, border to border, river to lake, a maddening canopy of darkness to the earliest settlers. There were a few places, however, where these earliest pioneers might emerge from the forest into an island of openness, an area that would restore for a while some peace of mind. But these islands of daylight that soothed the settlers were in a conflict of their own, a conflict that had been going on for hundreds of years before the first settlers arrived. Due to climatic changes, parts of western and northwestern Ohio would at one time be forest, at another a relatively treeless open savanna.

These openings were often called oak openings because of the hearty bur oak trees that ruled over the waving prairie grasses, thick barked trees that could survive raging prairie fires, trees with enormously deep taproots that could withstand drought. These groves of oaks and the prairies they oversaw were much like the great prairies of the west, the great prairie that just managed to reach this area of Ohio with what is called the Prairie Peninsula.

Of course, it was the forest that ultimately won the battle for turf in northwestern Ohio, and after the trees came the ax. Even the few remnants of the beautiful tall grass prairies in Ohio were eventually cut by the plow, yielding to corn and soybeans. It is rare indeed when even a small tract of prairie survives, perhaps along a railroad track, or shielded by stones in an old cemetery.

But in southwest Crawford County, along a country road, stands a 35 acre tract that has never seen the plow. Craggy, majestic, 300 year old bur oak trees, some solitary, some standing in groves, watch over sheep grazing beneath their boughs, sheep that return the favor by keeping out the invading plants that could ultimately spell the end of the delicately balanced savanna. For now, the passerby along this country road can enjoy a glimpse into a time long ago, and, like the settlers of two hundred years ago, perhaps gain some peace of mind.

POINTS OF INTEREST:

1. Nevada, Ohio
The loop begins in the village of Nevada, where food and drink are available. Pronounce it Ne-vay-da.

2. Broken Sword Creek
The creek flowing under this little metal bridge derives its name from the capture of Colonel William Crawford by the Indians two centuries ago. When Crawford was captured, he broke his sword upon the rocks along the creek bank so the weapon could not be used against him by the Indians. The Indians later gave the name Broken Sword to the stream. It is said that in 1889 a man planting corn along the creek bank found a sword like those worn by Revolutionary War officers, of which Crawford was one. It had a broken blade.

3. 1885 Schoolhouse
Built more than a century ago, this old brick schoolhouse has been out of service as a school for many years.

4. Swartz Covered Bridge
This historic bridge was built in 1880, using the Howe Truss design, and is one of only two covered bridges remaining in Wyandot County. The amount of graffiti on this bridge gives new meaning to the term "covered" bridge.

5. Pioneer Cemetery
Stones dating back to at least 1825 can be found in this early cemetery.

6. Daughmer Bur Oak Savanna
This 35 acre tract of virgin prairie sod and magnificent bur oak trees is in private hands, yet is clearly visible from the road as you pass by. A roadside historical marker describes the Sandusky Plains, of which this savanna was a part.

7. *The "Yankee Doodle" Bridge*
   This stately old metal truss bridge received a new look during the nation's bicentennial celebration, being painted red, white and blue, and further adorned with white stars on the vertical endposts. Although the paint has started to fade somewhat, it still looks rather snappy in its patriotic apparel.

8. *1890 Metal Bridge*
   This beautiful metal bridge, gleaming silver in the sunlight, spans the Sandusky River in an idyllic location. The bridge was built in 1890 by the Variety Iron Works Co. of Cleveland, Ohio.

9. *Route Note*
   Be sure you make *two* left turns as you pass through this intersection.

10. *Route Note*
    Use extra caution crossing busy SR 30 here and upon leaving Oceola.

11. *Oceola, Ohio*
    If you stop at the village sign as you enter the town from the north, and cast your gaze westward along the fencerow, you will see the woods where Frank, the War Horse, is buried. Frank, a Civil War cavalry horse, took part in an 87 day raid that covered seven states and more than 2,000 miles. After the war, he was popular at veterans' reunions, where he would recognize the flag and "prick up his ears at the sound of martial music". To this day, an occasional veteran will tramp back through the briars on the north side of the fencerow to decorate Frank's grave. His pink granite gravestone on a rise in the woods reads "Frank, The War Horse. Co A, 12 Regiment, O.C. Died 1886 at 28 years. From Atlanta to the Sea."

12. *Oceola United Brethren Cemetery*
    Located in this early cemetery beneath a spreading evergreen are the graves of several Civil War veterans, including at least two young men who died during the war. The figure of a Civil War soldier is sculpted into these two stones with the words "A Soldier of 1861" engraved into the white marble. A veteran of the Mexican War is also buried here.

NOTES/PHOTOS

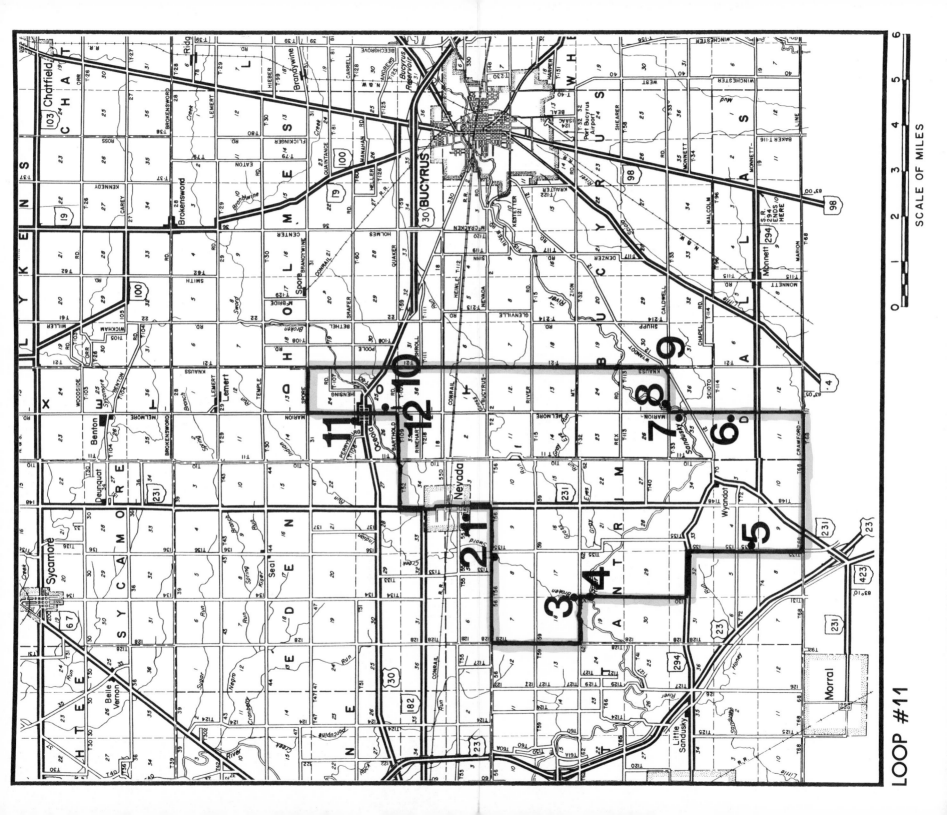

LOOP #11

SCALE OF MILES

LOOP #12

Length: 21 miles

Terrain: Flat to gently rolling

County: Auglaize

Top of the Canal

This 21 mile ride from Grand Lake St. Mary's takes the twentieth century traveler back more than one-hundred years to the days of the Miami and Erie Canal, the days of mules, mills, towpaths, and boom towns. Beginning at Grand Lake, which was the world's largest man-made reservoir and fed the canal, we travel south through two canal era towns, one still thriving, the other just surviving, past remnants of those romantic days, the brick canal houses and old locks. One-room schoolhouses from the turn of the century stand along the loop, and a stop at the ponds of the state's fish farm rounds out this ride through beautiful Auglaize County.

The flat to gently rolling terrain of western Auglaize County belies the fact that as you travel through this area, you are crossing a "great divide" known as the Loramie Summit, the highest point on the Miami and Erie Canal. This summit was 21 miles long, a plateau of water that was held in place by two locks, designated Number One South at Lockington and Number One North at New Bremen. From New Bremen, canal boats on the way to Cincinnati "locked down" 513 feet in vertical distance to the Ohio River; boats on the way to Toledo locked down 395 feet to Lake Erie. The north lock can be seen holding back water yet today in New Bremen, and a number of canal era buildings still stand near the old canal, giving us a glimpse of that by-gone era.

From Lock One we head north along the banks of the old canal through the village of Lock Two, Ohio. The prosperity and growth that characterized New Bremen gave promise to Lock Two as well, and the canal gave rise to a three story mill that stands at the Village Commons. The early miller's residence, now a private home, stands across from the mill, and the barn on the right as you enter the town served as a warehouse during the canal era. The large brick home and the old store across the Commons likewise date back to the canal days, being owned by John Garmhausen, who came to America from Germany in 1836. After seeking his fortune in California during the Gold Rush days, it seems that he "struck gold" here in Ohio along the waters of the old canal. As the canal waters vanished with the coming of the railroad, so did the prosperity of many of the towns that had sprung up along the "Big Ditch". Today, the mill is boarded up, and business life is virtually gone from Lock Two. Yet, it takes only a little imagination to look over to the banks and see the mules plodding along the towpaths, and to hear the rushing of the water as Lock Two empties and fills, a sound that transforms, if only in the mind, a ghost-like town back into the bustling canal town of a century ago.

Campers are advised that another day of exploring is available with the "Fort Amanda Ride", which also departs from Grand Lake St. Mary's State Park.

POINTS OF INTEREST:

1. *Grand Lake St. Mary's State Park*
   The ride begins at the East Embankment picnic area at the east end of the lake just south of the railroad tracks. Cyclists may want to follow the park road south along the shore of the lake, then cut over to SR 364 at the end of the park road. To reach the park's camping and swimming areas, enter off of nearby SR 364/703 west.

2. *Feeder Canal*
   After your turn onto CR 114A, you will ride alongside the old feeder canal that carried water from the reservoir into the canal system. American water lilies now blossom in the canal.

3. *One-Room Schoolhouse*
   This ornate old brick schoolhouse, long out of service, stands on private property at the terminus of Waesch Rd.

4. *1902 Schoolhouse*
   At the top of a gentle rise stands this early one-room schoolhouse, its bell tower, complete with bell, silhouetted against the sky. School days are over for this beautiful building, and it has been converted into a private residence.

5. *New Bremen, Ohio*
   Follow the "local truck route" signs through the streets of this charming village, past the museum and other early brick homes. Turn left at SR 274 (Monroe St.) to pass through the quaint business section on your

way to the canal lock, which is located on the south side of Monroe St. at Washington Street. In front of the library on S. Washington is the historical marker describing the lock. Leaving town by going north on Jefferson St. (New Bremen-New Knoxville Rd.) from Monroe St., you will pass by a canal house built in 1853 that faces the old canal. The museum on N. Main is open Sundays April-Sept., 1 to 4.

6. *Lock Two, Ohio*

7. *Route Note*
   Use extra caution on this short stretch of SR 66. A berm is available for cyclists.

8. *St. Mary's Fish Farm*
   Fifty-two acres of ponds are located here at the state's fish farm, where pike, bass, and other fish are raised. As you ride slowly along the dikes between the ponds, you will observe many waterfowl and shore birds, especially during the seasonal migrations of spring and fall. Visiting hours are 9 to 4.

NOTES/PHOTOS

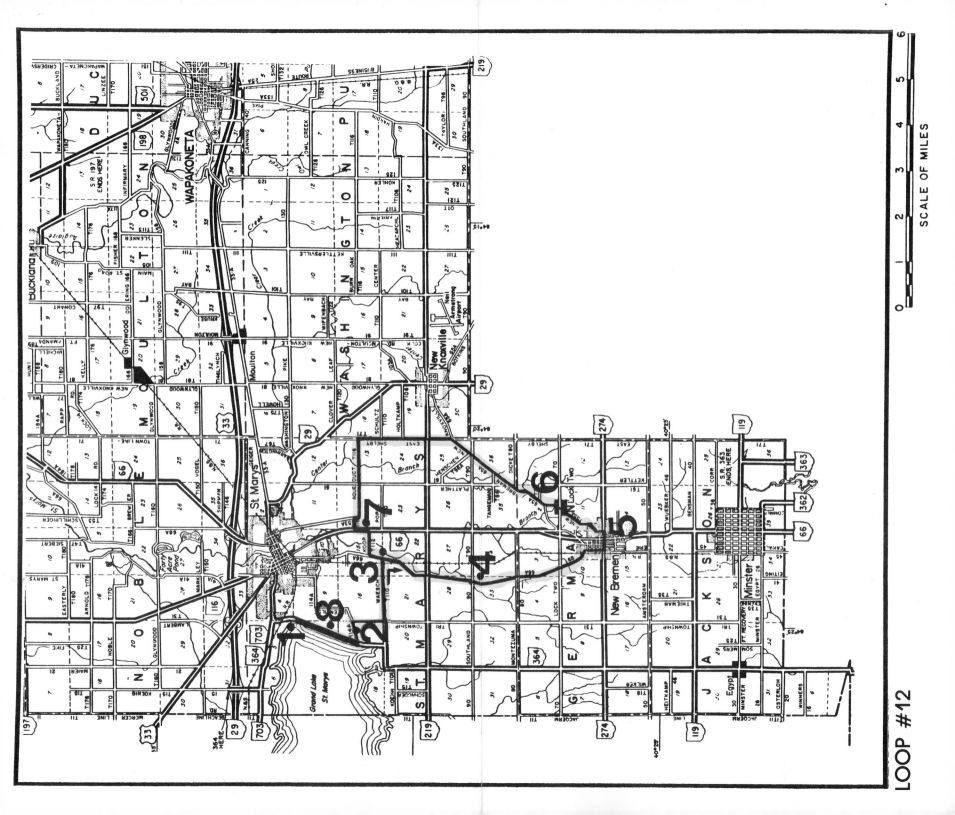

LOOP #12

SCALE OF MILES

0 1 2 3 4 5 6

LOOP #13

Length: 42 miles

Terrain: Flat to gently rolling

County: Auglaize

The Fort Amanda Ride

This 42 mile ride through northwest Auglaize County winds along quiet country roads, past peaceful ponds and over old metal bridges on the way to the site of Fort Amanda, which played an important role in the War of 1812. Along the way are one room schoolhouses, brick country churches, and vestiges of the old Miami and Erie Canal, including one canal feature so spectacular it is on the National Register of Historic Places.

It has been said that cemeteries are history books of stone, and our visit to the site of Fort Amanda brings to life an important chapter in Ohio's turbulent past. Northwest Ohio had been a battleground during the 1790's, as three American generals had tried to defeat the Indians and open the area for settlement. It took only eight years from Anthony Wayne's victory at Fallen Timbers for Ohio to become the 17th state, and after only nine years of statehood, Ohio again became a battleground. The War of 1812 in Ohio was a war waged not only against the British, but against the Indians of Tecumseh's Federation as well. Fort Amanda was constructed by General William Henry Harrison in 1812 to protect the supply lines that reached north to the Maumee Rapids, and the fort also served as a hospital for wounded soldiers returning from the front.

Today, the site of the old fort is marked by a 50 foot high obelisk, and the path leading to the memorial takes us past the 1814 U.S. Cemetery where 75 soldiers who died at the fort are buried. When the British burned the War Records Office in Washington, D.C. in 1814, the identities of these countrymen were forever lost. The white military markers of these Unknown Soldiers read simply, "U.S. Soldier, War of 1812". Another marker testifying to the Indian aspect of the war is inscribed "Capt. E. Dawson, Murdered by Indians, Oct. 1812", and an earlier veteran from the Revolutionary War, William Taylor of the New Jersey Militia, is also buried here.

Heroic deeds are, of course, not limited to war and strife. The traveler along this route will pass by an epic feat of another kind, a feature simply called "Deep Cut". Carved by hand through the dirt and rock, this 6,600 foot long cut on the Miami and Erie Canal is one of the most spectacular hand-excavated canal projects ever undertaken, and has earned a place in the National Register of Historic Places. Today, Deep Cut serves as a memorial to the industriousness and perseverance of the early builders of Ohio.

Campers are advised that another day of exploring is available with the "Top of the Canal Ride", also departing from Grand Lake St. Marys.

POINTS OF INTEREST:

1. *Grand Lake St. Marys State Park*
   The ride begins at this state park, where camping, swimming, and picnicking are available. Use extra caution on the road leading from the park.

2. *Forty Acre Pond*
   Travelers seeking a quiet spot for reflection will enjoy passing by this serene pond, a wide water of the old canal.

3. *1895 Metal Bridge*

4. *Metal Bridge*

5. *Route Note*
   Cyclists are advised to use extra caution when traveling along or crossing state routes such as SR 197, 66, and 198.

6. *Miami and Erie Canal*
   You will be traveling along a water-filled section of the Miami and Erie Canal as you head north along CR 66A.

7. *Deep Cut*
   The Cut is visible from the little bridge on Deep Cut Road over the canal, and a roadside park on the west side of SR 66 provides another view of the canal and towpath here.

8. *1885 Schoolhouse*
   For the hard working German immigrants of the late 19th century, this was the place many of them first learned to speak the language of their new country. The land on which the school stands was once purchased by a Mr. Fischer for a pair of leather boots. It is now private property.

9. *Fort Amanda Historical Site*
   Operated by The Ohio Historical Society, the site is open daily. Picnic tables are located at the site.

10. *Metal Bridge*

11. *Glynwood, Ohio*
    An 1883 brick country church and an 1899 one room schoolhouse stand at the intersection in the crossroads town of Glynwood.

NOTES/PHOTOS

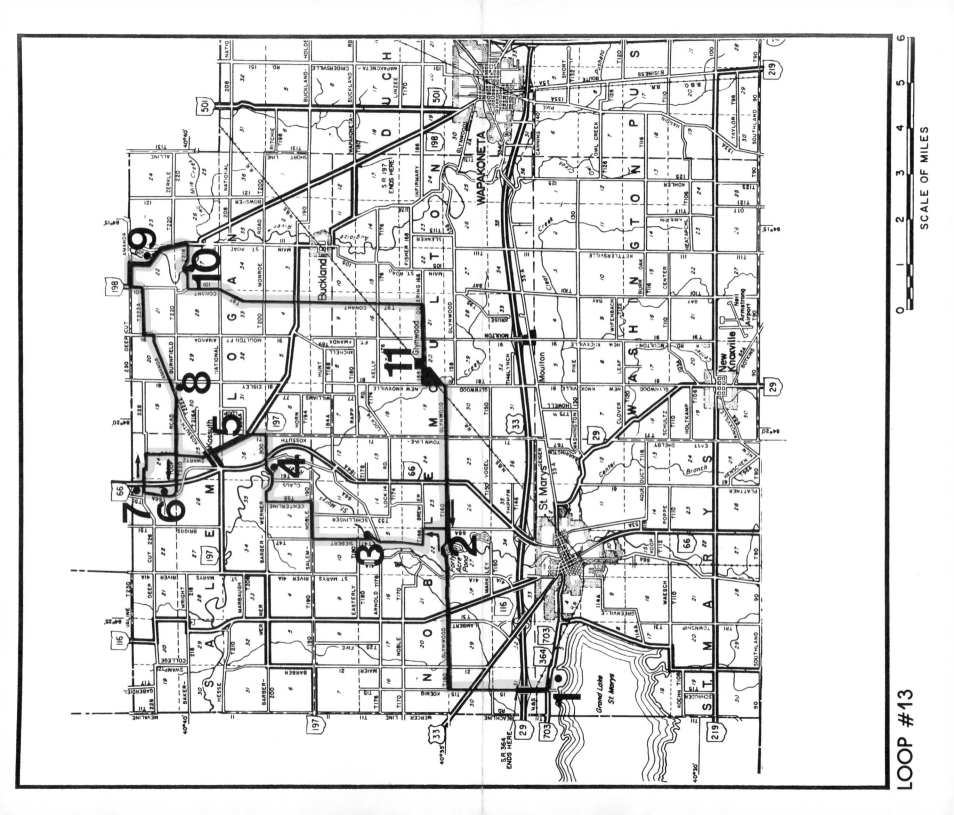

LOOP #13

SCALE OF MILES

LOOP #14

Length: 31 miles

Terrain: Flat

County: Wood

Red Barn Country

This 31 mile ramble through the countryside of Wood County meanders along the banks of the beautiful Portage River before passing through an early metal bridge that serves as a gateway to the fields and farms of this red barn country. Egrets and herons can be seen standing in the riffles of the river, and golden rolls of hay dot the summertime fields along these country roads. In addition to simply enjoying this pastoral scene, the traveler along this loop can visit the grave of one of the famous Andrews Raiders of Civil War fame and tour the Old Infirmary, built well over a century ago as the county's "poor house". Now the home of the Wood County museum, exhibits of nineteenth century living, ranging from the macabre to the quaint, are housed in the old institution.

There are few scenes more enchanting to the backroad explorer than those featuring big red barns and golden fields. Perhaps it is because our national heritage is rooted on the farm that we have a sense of coming home when we travel these narrow country lanes, passing by the old homesteads, clothes hanging on the line and a tire swing dangling from a tree. Although life on the farm today is far from idyllic, and involves seemingly unending work, something was added to the landscape here a little more than 50 years ago that changed life on the farm in a dramatic fashion. Now taken for granted and little noticed by the passerby, the coming of the wooden utility poles was eagerly watched and anticipated by the farm families of the 1930's. Because running lines to the isolated farms was not cost efficient for the power companies of the day, farmers formed co-ops, and with the assistance of the federal government, began setting the poles and stringing the lines that brought an end to much of the drudgery of farm work.

The day the lights came on in the country was not a day without problems, however. Like anything else, it took some getting used to. According to the Ohio Rural Electric Cooperatives, one woman used a pot holder to turn on her light switches, while another kept her outlets plugged to keep the electricity from draining out. The Rural Electric Administration received a letter from another woman who, although quite pleased with the electricity, had trouble sleeping with the light on in her bedroom. She was instructed in how to operate the switch on the wall. And what was the most desired appliance after electricity came? The electric washing machine topped the list.

Finally, the traveler along the loop will see barns of various sizes and shapes, including the beautiful bank barn, named for the dirt bank that leads up to the second floor. Animals entered their quarters on the first floor on the side opposite the bank in such barns. Bank barns originated in the mountainous country of Pennsylvania, but were so efficient that they were adopted even in the flatlands. Roof styles also vary from barn to barn, and the "bent-roof" design seen on many barns in rural Ohio is called "gambrel". Following a visit to the Old Infirmary, the sharp-eyed scout will spot a beautiful barn combining the gambrel roof and bank design standing along the loop.

With the magnificent barns, scenic river, old bridges, and, yes, even wooden utility poles, this ride through the countryside is truly a tonic for the harried.

POINTS OF INTEREST:

1. *William Henry Harrison Park*
   The loop begins at this county park located on Pemberville Road (Bierley Rd.) at the southern boundary of Pemberville. Picnic tables, restrooms, and drinking water are available here, and the park is open daily.

2. *Route Note*
   Be cautious as you cross busy SR 6.

3. *1898 Metal Bridge*
   Built by the Canton Bridge Builders nearly a century ago, this old bridge spans the Portage River.

4. *Route Note*
   Pass straight through this intersection both times, making this a "figure-eight" loop.

5. *The Old Infirmary*

Home to the Wood County Historical Society, the museum is open for tours Wed, Thur, and Fri 12-4, and Sunday 1-4. There is an admission charge of $1.00 for adults.

6. *Paupers Cemetery*

A lone marker stands by the road south of the Old Infirmary, marking the old paupers cemetery. All the other markers, which bore only a number and no name, were removed from here in the 1950's.

7. *Route Note*

County Home Road makes a right jog over the freeway at Kramer Road.

8. *Grave of Elihu Mason*

A marker stands at the main Pemberville Cemetery entrance, describing the feats of Mason and his fellow Raiders. His gray obelisk marker is located just a few stones southwest of the center crossroads in the cemetery. The crossroads are marked by a single tree standing at the juncture.

9. *Pemberville, Ohio*

After entering the town, turn right on Bridge Street at the 1902 Township Hall, then right on Bierley Rd. to return to the park.

NOTES/PHOTOS

LOOP #14

SCALE OF MILES

To guide your further explorations into the Ohio Country, Backroad Chronicles offers more *Life In The Slow Lane* by Jeff and Nadean DiSabato Traylor:

ORDER BLANK/MAILING LIST

Please send _____ copies of *Life In The Slow Lane* at $9.95 plus $2.00 tax and postage per copy.

Please specify edition:

☐ Central Ohio

☐ Southwest Ohio

☐ Northwest Ohio

☐ Please add my name to your mailing list for future editions.

Name _____

Address _____

City _____ State _____ Zip _____

Mail order blank and payment to:

Backroad Chronicles
P.O. Box 292066
Columbus, OH 43229